D0251188

MY THERAPIST SAID

The author before he got depressed.

MY THERAPIST SAID

poems by

HAL SIROWITZ

Crown Publishers, Inc.

New York

The author would like to thank the following colonies, which awarded him residencies to work on this book: the MacDowell Colony, Ragdale Foundation, Vermont Studio Center, and Virginia Center for the Creative Arts.

"I Finally Managed to Speak to Her" appeared previously in *Aloud: Voices from the Nuyorican Poets Cafe* (Henry Holt) and will also appear in *Poetry in Motion—100 Poems on the Subways and Buses, Vol. 2* (W.W. Norton). "Mother Talks to the Dead" appeared previously in *Chelsea*. "J. C. Penney" appeared previously in *Response*. "Subject Matter" appeared previously in *Mudfish*. "The Room Was Cold" appeared previously in *Ploplop*. "Why the Violin Is Better," "The Right Advice," "Forever & Ever," and "Knowing Your Role" will appear in *Identity Lessons: Learning American Style* (Viking Penguin).

Copyright © 1998 by Hal Sirowitz

Published by Crown Publishers, Inc., 201 East 50th Street, New York, New York 10022. Member of the Crown Publishing Group.

Random House, Inc. New York, Toronto, London, Sydney, Auckland www.randomhouse.com

CROWN and colophon are trademarks of Crown Publishers, Inc.

Printed in the United States of America

Library of Congress Cataloging-in-Publication Data
Sirowitz, Hal.
    My therapist said / Hal Sirowitz.
    I. Title.
PS3569.I725M9   1998   97-18191
811'.54—dc21   CIP

ISBN 609-60130-x

10   9   8   7   6   5   4   3   2   1

First Edition

To my therapists, who had to put up with
my mother's phone calls when she
thought I wasn't improving fast enough.
And to Dennis Nurkse.

CONTENTS

THEY ALL HAVE BOYFRIENDS

If you ask a woman if she has
a boyfriend, my therapist said, she's
going to say yes, even if she doesn't
have one, because she doesn't want you
to think of her as a loner. And even if
she has more than one boyfriend, it's not
a waste of your time being with her,
because you need more practice talking
to women. All that time you spent
talking with your mother doesn't count.

FREEDOM MEANS
NOTHING TO LOSE

When you knew your father was dying,
my therapist said, you thought if you
got married it'd please him. So
you got into some painful relationships.
You were ready to get married
until you got dropped. But now
that he's dead you're free. You don't
have to marry anyone. You can get
into painful relationships just for the hell of it.

LONELY DAYS, LONELY NIGHTS

When I asked you what you did
last week, my therapist said, you said
you did nothing. So I can't understand
how you can tell me that this week
you did even less. You
must have at least gone to the store.
And even if you bought nothing,
the fact that you left the house
so your mother couldn't nag you is something.

PSYCHOLOGY BOOKS

Some therapists don't let their patients
read Freud, my therapist said. But
you can read as many of his books
as you like. You can read
Horney, Adler, & Jung, too.
I read some of their books. I'm not
afraid of the competition. They can
never be as good as I am at telling you
what you need to do. They never knew you.

SUBJECT MATTER

The reason you don't have much
to talk about, my therapist said, is
because you're not doing anything. If I
stayed in my room all day, I'd have
nothing to talk about, either. You should
go to a dance, & even if you don't meet anyone,
you can at least describe to me what it was like,
which I'd find interesting, because I don't
go out anymore. I'm not trying to sway you.
If you insist on talking about nothing,
I'd still listen, but I'm convinced you'll be
much happier if you had something to talk about.

NO LOVE LOST BETWEEN THEM

Mothers don't like therapists,
my therapist said. If their child
is seeing one, then they're afraid
that they're getting criticized
for things they did fifteen years ago.
And I am very critical
of your mother, but never
to her face. You're the one
who keeps telling her what
I said. So I can understand
why she has to dislike me.

CLOSING YOUR EARS

Your mother called me, my therapist said,
& was very concerned about you. She said
you look lifeless. I told her you've
been making great progress. She said
that I must be crazy. I told her that I'm
a psychiatrist. I can't be crazy. Then she
told me about this crazy psychiatrist she heard
on the radio. I just let her talk. I realized
it was useless to argue with her.
And that's what you should do. Just because
someone is talking doesn't mean that you have
        to listen.

GETTING THROUGH TO
YOUR THERAPIST

Your therapist is always going to take
your side, Mother said, because you're
her patient. So if I wanted my side
to be heard, I'd have to get my own therapist.
Then my therapist could call yours
& tell her my complaints about you.
I heard doctors listen to one another
more than they listen to ordinary people.
But I couldn't afford to do that,
because we've already been paying for yours.

NOT NORMAL

When you were in the second grade,
Mother said, the school asked us to take you
to a psychologist. He saw you
for a while. Then he told us to discontinue
the visits, because you appeared to be normal.
We had no reason not to believe him.
But now we're not too sure. It isn't
normal to want to wear an undershirt
with holes in it. And when we throw it
away, you brood about it for days. You should
be happy that we can afford to buy you new ones.

DON'T TALK BACK

There are two sides to every story,
Mother said, but since I'm the adult
& you're the child, only my side counts.
Yours will count, too, one of these days,
but right now your job is to listen,
so when it's your turn to be a parent
& your child tries to interrupt you
while you're speaking, you'll know what to say.

OUR SECRET

If you laugh, Mother said, the world
laughs with you, but if you cry,
not only will the world not cry with you
but everyone will want to leave
the room, because no one wants
to get a headache by being next
to a crybaby. So I'm going
to give you a tissue. I want
you to wipe your eyes & throw it
away. Then no one else will
know that you cried unless
you're dumb enough to tell someone.

COPING WITH YOUR DAD

It wouldn't be so bad if you were paying
some therapist, Father said, to help you cope
with your parents. But to make me pay
for someone to tell you how to give me
a tough time doesn't make any sense. I
can tell you how to do it. And I won't
charge you anything, because you're my son.
Never be afraid of me. I'm not that bad.
I know plenty of fathers who are much worse.
I might yell at you, but I'll never kick you
out of the house. I'm not your enemy.
I can't be. We have the same blood.

ANOTHER GIRLFRIEND GONE

A girlfriend doesn't break up with a guy,
Father said, for no reason. You must have
done something wrong. She had to have
a reason. Maybe she didn't like the way
you dress. I kept telling you to wear a jacket
& tie. I didn't even know her, but already
I'm taking her side, because I do know you.
I thought she might have been the one
you were going to marry. I was all ready
to welcome her into the family. I guess
I'll just have to welcome someone else.

THE CLOTHES WE BOUGHT YOU

Your mother & I bought you some nice clothes,
Father said, but we never saw you wear them.
I was too polite to say anything about it
until now. If they're still in the box,
they're not doing you any good. A woman
isn't going to ask you if she can visit
your apartment to check out your wardrobe.
She's going to make a judgment about you
based on what you're wearing at that moment.
And if she decides you don't know how
to dress right, she'll think that there must be
other things you don't know how to do, too, & she'll
    drop you.

THE FIRST HURDLE

She said that her therapist approved
of me. I felt like I passed the first test.
Now all I needed was for her to like me.

STILL LIFE

Green bananas on her table.
Will she sleep with me
before they turn ripe
or will I, like the fruit flies,
have to wait for the next bunch?

I FINALLY MANAGED TO
SPEAK TO HER

She was sitting across from me
on the bus. I said, "The trees
look so much greener in this part
of the country. In New York City
everything looks so drab." She said,
"It looks the same to me. Show me
a tree that's different." "That one,"
I said. "Which one?" she said.
"It's too late," I said; "we already
passed it." "When you find another one,"
she said, "let me know." And then
she went back to reading her book.

MOTHER DISAPPROVAL

She said that her mother wouldn't
like me because I was Jewish.
That didn't bother me. Her mother
wasn't the one I wanted to sleep with.

HER REASON NOT TO

We were sitting on her bed.
She said she didn't believe
in sex. I didn't need her
to believe in it. I just
wanted her to do it.

THE FAME GAME

You have this need to be famous,
my therapist said, but I think
you should get a job first. If
you look at all the famous people,
they all had jobs. George Bush
never looks like he's doing anything,
but he was once a President. You have
to start from somewhere. Otherwise
you'll just be famous inside
your own head, but so is everyone else.

I AM WHAT I AM

Even if you were rich & famous,
my therapist said, you still wouldn't
make her happy. She'd keep asking you,
"Are you sure you're famous?" And
you'll have to keep saying, "Yes.
I am." But that won't stop her from thinking
that you might be tricking her. She
doesn't have faith in people. She's
always going to think you're someone else.

THE SIX O'CLOCK NEWS

She broke up with you the same way
David Brinkley reads the news,
my therapist said. She gave you
the reasons why you & she weren't
compatible; then she moved on
to something else, to the next story.
But for you the breakup was the only story,
because you experienced it firsthand.

UNLIKE MOSES

She went to her parents on her only vacation
instead of spending it with you,
my therapist said. She wasn't like Moses,
who went to Mount Sinai after he left
his people. At least he got something done.
He spoke to God. She only spoke to her aunt.
He gave the world the Ten Commandments.
All she did was argue with her family.
Then she returned to argue with you.
But she was doing that before she went away.

BOTH WANTING TO LISTEN

You read in a book that the best way
to get someone attracted to you,
my therapist said, is to be a good listener.
But the problem is that she read the same book.
So while you're trying to get her to talk,
she only wants to listen. Therefore she's
not becoming attracted to you, & you're not
getting attracted to her, because
neither of you is saying anything.

TANGIBLE EVIDENCE

Just because she started the letter
calling you *dear*, my therapist said,
& ended it with *love* doesn't mean
that she has a crush on you. Millions
of people start & end a letter that way.
If you were a detective, you'd never
solve a case, because you'd fall for
the first phony clue that the murderer left you.
You have to wait for her to write
another letter to tell if she likes you. And
even then you might not have enough proof.

THE LIBIDO METHOD OF COUNTING

You told me you weren't going to sleep with her
until the fifth date, my therapist said,
but now you claim that since you spent
a night at her place without sex,
that should count for at least three dates,
& the next time you see her you'll sleep with her.
It sounds like you're letting your libido
do the counting. You told me
you wanted to go step by step, but
now you're taking three steps at a time.

ANSWERS TO QUESTIONS

Don't become serious with a woman,
Mother said, until I get a chance
to meet her. There are some questions
I can ask that you can't, like "Why
are you marrying him when you can
marry someone who dresses a lot neater?"
And if she tells me that you're very neat,
I'll know that she's crazy & is
probably the right woman for you.

BIG BAD WOLF

You should fall in love without leaving
your feet, Mother said. Your toes should
always be touching the ground. When
I fell in love with your father, I didn't
hear bells, but heard the gritting
of teeth. He was a wolf. His paws
were always slipping over my shoulders.
When I tried to tame him by twisting
his fingers, he'd get drunk
on cheap red wine & throw up on my shoes.

THE LAST DAYS

We know you don't think we're good parents,
Mother said. You blame us for whatever goes wrong
in your life. But we're the best scapegoats
you're ever going to have. Your wife
won't be as obliging. Don't you realize
if you blame her, she'll blame you?
Then what are you going to do, get a divorce?
If you do, don't think you can come back
& live with us. We're not that stupid.
Once we get rid of you, it'll be for keeps.
Of course we'll let you visit. If
the weather is bad that night, you can sleep over.
But in the morning you'll have to go.

NO EXPLANATION NEEDED

I don't have to give you a reason,
Mother said. If I say you can't
go outside after dinner, then you can't.
A policeman has to tell you why he's
giving you a ticket. But I don't have
to give you any explanations for my actions.
It's one of the perks of my job,
& I see no reason for changing it. But
if you cleaned your room, like you
promised me you would, not only
would you understand why I'm punishing you,
you'd also be able to go outside.

THE RIGHT ADVICE

Don't ask your mother for advice about women,
Father said. She's a woman, so she can't
be objective. She'll stick up for her kind.
I'm a man, so I can't be objective, either,
but that'll never stop me from giving you
the right advice. If a woman wants
to sleep with you, then you should do it.
Don't be a fool & ask yourself if you're
really in love with her. That's what your mother
would tell you to do. And that's why
the only man she ever slept with was me.

TOUCHING BOTTOM

When you go swimming, don't go out so far,
where you can't touch bottom, Father said.
It's good to know it's there even if you don't
use it. Why do you think I got married?
Do you really think I need your mother?
I did it because I knew someday I'd
get old & tired. I had to have a place
where if I wanted to I could rest.

ERASING THOSE YEARS

I lied to your mother about my age,
Father said, when I first met her. I
knew I was older than she, so
I made myself ten years younger.
There were plenty of years in my life
that I didn't want to remember,
so I just forgot about those, & made
my childhood more current. On
our honeymoon I told her the truth.
I figured by that time it was
too late for her to do anything about it.

DARK RED

I thought this was my lucky lipstick,
she said, because I was wearing it
when I met you. But now that you
turned out to be not so nice,
I'm going to get rid of it. I wish
it was as easy to get rid of you.

MIRROR LOOKING

You're a little narcissistic, she said.
At the restaurant I kept noticing
you looking in the mirror. But
I knew that once you saw me naked,
that'd make you stop looking at yourself.

THE WAIT

You make love the old-fashioned way,
she said. You didn't take off your clothes.
I was glad you left mine on, too. Humping
is a lost art. You're one of the few men
I know who practices it. I wasn't ready
for anything more serious. I look
forward to seeing you next week,
but don't be disappointed if I'm
still not ready. I don't know
how long it'll take. It could be
a month or it might take longer.
But once I start, I won't stop.

WE WERE PUTTING ON A SHOW

I was kissing your neck in the park.
You said the couple sitting across from us
was watching the whole time. But they
definitely weren't learning anything. They kept
sitting there not touching, with their arms folded.

WHAT DOES SHE KNOW

She's wrong to accuse you of being addicted
to sex, my therapist said. First,
you haven't had enough sex to become
addicted to it. And second, she
hasn't slept with you, so she doesn't know.
Right now it's only her opinion. It's
true that you talk about it a lot,
but that's mainly because you're not
doing it. I predict that as soon as you
sleep with someone again you'll shut up about it.

STOLEN BED

I don't think her last boyfriend stole
her bed, my therapist said. I think
it was just an excuse she made so
she wouldn't have to take you back
to her apartment. He could have stolen
her pillow. That's more plausible. But
the important point here is that she
likes to make her life into a drama.
And you may not get more than a walk-on role.

KING OVER THE QUEEN

When she told you that she doesn't sleep
with a guy until the fifth date,
my therapist said, & you told her that you
could wait until the sixth one, because
you weren't in a rush, I don't think
that made her happy. You were
supposed to talk her down, not lengthen
the amount of time you had to wait.
You lost points by being too agreeable.
It was like she was playing cards
with you, & when she showed you
her queen, you were supposed to
counter with a king, & not give up your turn.

THE CLOCK STRUCK TWELVE

You made a mistake not going back
to her place, my therapist said. You
can't just tell her you're tired.
She's going to think you're not interested.
The only way you'll be able to sleep
with her is if you stay up real late,
because that tells her you like her.
It's not like you're going to turn
into a pumpkin. That only happened
in "Cinderella." And even she slept
with the prince. It's not mentioned
directly. But what else do you
think living happily ever after means?

THE NUMBER FACTOR

Just because she slept with forty guys,
my therapist said, doesn't mean she's
great at sex. It could mean she has
trouble sustaining a relationship. It depends
on the perspective you take.
And I'm not sure you'd be happy
being number forty-one. I'd be distrustful
of anyone who is too much into numbers.
You have to ask yourself, do you want
a relationship, or do you just want to be on
        someone's list.

WAITING FOR YOUR TURN

Sex is something you're supposed to be
doing together, my therapist said. But
if she's just touching your private parts,
& once in a while she lets you touch hers,
then you're just watching each other.
It's almost like you're playing
Scrabble on two separate boards.
Neither of you can win or lose.

SEX SLAVE

She told you to close your eyes,
my therapist said, but when you
opened them, it wasn't the present
you expected. It was a pair
of handcuffs. And she wasn't
going to offer to take turns,
or lock you to her. She
just wanted to lock you to her bed.
I'm glad you said no. She might
never have let you go. You might
have missed our appointment.

IT'S BETTER TO WAIT

I hope you never take advantage of women
like your father did, Mother said. He didn't
take advantage of me, because I didn't
let him. And just because you can sleep
with a woman doesn't mean you have to.
You should wait until you're married.
Then you'll have something to look forward to.
Otherwise you'll be bored with each other.
You won't know what to do on your wedding night.
You won't want to have sex, because you did that
        already.

FOREVER & EVER

I overheard your father giving you advice
about women, Mother said. Don't listen
to him. He's no expert. The only reason
we stayed married so long was because
I don't believe in divorce. I always
told myself that when I got married
it would last forever. Then I told him.

STRAY DOG

I'm telling your sister my life story,
Father said. All of a sudden she
starts looking at a dog in her backyard,
& wants me to look at it, too. But
my life is a lot more interesting
than any dog. I survived the Great Depression.
I supported both of my parents. And
what did that dog do? It got loose.
It ran away from the neighbor's house.
Big deal. I could have done that, too.
But I stayed home to help my mom & dad.

FAMILY GRAVE

This is where my parents are buried,
Father said. This is your grandmother.
That's your grandfather. I wish
they could see me standing here right now.
Then they would finally have to appreciate me.
I'm the only one who comes. Your aunt
doesn't want to be bothered. She's too busy
chasing men. I tell her there's no reason
she can't bring them here. She said
none of them are interested in meeting a dead family.

IN THE DICTIONARY

Just like there are two sides to a penny,
Father said, Lincoln on one side,
the memorial on the other, I happen
to have more than one side. So I
apologize for yelling at you. You
caught me at an off moment. And
you have to stop being so sensitive.
I'm supposed to yell at you. It's
part of my job description. And if
you don't believe me, you should look up
the word *father* in the dictionary.
I'm certain it says that we're supposed
to be mean sometimes, & if it doesn't say that,
then I'll have to buy you a better edition.

BAD RECEPTION

I thought about you
while I was masturbating.
Then I thought about her.
It was like switching channels
on the television set.
I'd have stayed with you,
but her picture was clearer.

A NEW TOY

She handed me a condom.
But by the time I opened it
I wasn't able to use it.
A little later I saw her cat
playing with it. I was glad
someone got some use out of it.

SAFETY IN LOVE

She took off my pants, grabbed hold
of my penis, & said, "Should I do it
fast or slow?" "Fast," I said. Then I
realized I shouldn't be in such a rush.
But by that time it was already too late.

THE ROOM WAS COLD

She said she didn't know me well enough
to sleep with me, so she jerked me off instead.
Sperm got in my eye. It stayed shut
for a while. She said she was sorry
for not being able to do anything right.
But it wasn't like there was a lot to see.
I was the only one who was naked.

GIVING IT A REST

I don't think you should be mad at her,
my therapist said, if she wants to do other things
besides spending the whole day with you in bed.
Even I'm getting tired of hearing you tell me,
week after week, about how wonderful sex is.
It's fun when you first do it. Then
it's supposed to reach a plateau. I
think you're afraid that the relationship
is going to end, so you keep insisting
that she sleep with you all the time,
because you'll know how lonely you'll be
without her. But sex won't prevent the ending
from happening. All it'll do is keep sending
you back to the store to buy more condoms.

ACHIEVING CLOSURE

You're both trying to achieve closure
in this relationship, my therapist said.
You want to marry her. She wants
to break up with you. And I think
she's going to prevail, because
it's a lot easier for her to break up
with you than it is for you
to marry her. You'll have to buy her
a ring, go for a blood test, & get
both families involved. All she has
to do is not see you again. And
it seems like she has already started doing that.

DANCING THE SAME DANCE

You keep having arguments with her,
my therapist said. She tells you
to leave. You leave. Then she wants
you back. It's like a dance.
Aren't you tired of doing the same
cha cha cha month after month? Don't
you think it's time you learned
a new step, like the tango? If she
won't learn it with you, then
you'll just have to get another partner.

SO-SO RELATIONSHIP

It seems like she falls into patterns,
my therapist said. She has
a serious relationship. Then she
has a so-so one. Unfortunately for you,
she met you right after she had
a serious one. If you had known
about her patterns, you could have told her,
Please get your so-so relationship
out of the way; then call me when
you're ready for a serious one. But
you didn't know. And she didn't tell.

COMPLETING THE EQUATION

It doesn't take you long to fall
in love with someone, my therapist said.
With your last girlfriend it only
took you two seconds. On a cold day
it takes longer to start a car. The
Jefferson Airplane have this line,
"Why don't you find somebody to love?"
And that's what you've been doing.
But you're only completing half of the equation.
You keep forgetting that it'll be a lot more
fun if you find someone who loves you back.

NOT A GOOD START

To take you to a gay bar on the first date,
my therapist said, doesn't sound like
she had a lot of experience going out
with men. You must have found it difficult
when she went to the bathroom & left you
alone & you had to explain
to this man why you weren't available.
She might have been trying to make
a point—that not all men need
to sleep with women. If she was,
then she shouldn't have been hurt
when you never asked her out again.

SEX AMONG THE COATS

She must have found it sexually exciting
at the party, my therapist said, to take
you into the coatroom, shut the door,
& pull down your pants. But when
two women kept knocking on the door to get
their coats, you must have found it
very frustrating, because she couldn't
finish what she started. Plus, when
you & she walked out of the room,
it was you who got the dirty looks.

HEADLESS NUDE

If she showed you her painting
of her last boyfriend, my therapist said,
& he had no head, then maybe she's
trying to tell you something in paint
that she can't say in words—that she's
only interested in having a physical relationship.
I don't think you have to worry about
the possibility of her actually chopping off
your head, but you should be aware
that if she also does a portrait of you
in the nude, you shouldn't spend a lot
of energy holding your head still, because
that's probably not what she's painting.

AFTER THE BATHROOM

If I came back from the bathroom,
my therapist said, & saw my date
talking to another guy, I'd try not
to go again, which wouldn't be easy to do,
especially after I'd been drinking beer.
You don't want to be developing
any future bladder problems. And I'd
be annoyed, too, if after I sat down
she told me how smart he must have been
to have become an electrical engineer.
I wouldn't care what he did. I'd
just have been concerned about how big
he was, in case I had to fight him.

WAITING ROOM

Having your girlfriend wait in my office,
my therapist said, so I'd get a chance
to see what she looks like, was not
a good idea. I can't get a good impression
of her just by looking at her. I needed
to have talked to her. And when she
asks you what I thought about her,
tell her that I liked her a lot. Then
let her know she shouldn't have been
ripping pages out of my magazines.

MISSING SOCKS

You're lucky she never called you back,
my therapist said, especially after she
bragged about flushing her last boyfriend's socks
down the toilet. Not only might she have
messed up your plumbing, she wouldn't have
respected your property. You need
to find someone who has more appropriate
ways of expressing her anger. You wouldn't
like it if the day after you & she had a fight
you had to count your socks
each time you looked into your drawer.

BLIND FAITH

Sleeping with your father got me you,
Mother said, & you weren't the prize
I thought you'd be. It's a pity I can't
return you, give you back to the hospital,
& say, He can't be my son; you must have
given me the wrong baby, because he
hates everything good I do for him.
They'll ask me why I didn't return you
right away, & when I tell them I had faith
in you, that you'd eventually turn out good,
despite the fact that you ate with your mouth open
after I constantly told you to close it,
they'll look at me as if I was a fool.

THE COW OVER THE MOON

If a cow could jump over the moon,
Mother said, while a cat played
the fiddle, just think of what
I could do if you practiced
playing your violin every day. I could clean
the house faster. The cow didn't
have to beg the cat to play, like I
have to do with you. If you meet
a nice girl & she plays an instrument
& you don't, she won't want to go out
with you, because you won't have
much in common. The more hobbies
you have, the more women you'll meet.

LIFE TERM

Being a parent is like a prison term,
Mother said. You're a mother for life.
I knew I'd be stuck with you, but
what angers me is that you act like
you're stuck with me. If you don't appreciate me,
why don't you ask some of your friends' mothers
if they'll let you live with them, & you'll
be surprised at how fast they say no.
Even if you murdered someone & your picture
appeared on the front page of every newspaper
in the country, I wouldn't stop being
your mother. I'd just tell all the reporters
that you never learned how to be violent from me.

E-STRING TATTOO

When I play my violin, Father said,
the songs are only as good as the string marks.
My mother had to chase me around the house
with a broomstick to make me practice.
Now my fingers are as tattooed with E strings
as my arms once were with bruises.
Yet I remember her more than my father.
He was like the spaces between my fingers,
but she squeezed music out of them.

FOOLING THE DENTIST

My dentist would look out the window
to see what kind of car I had, Father said.
If I had an expensive car, he'd charge me
a fortune. So one day I parked
two blocks from his office. He spent an hour
working on my teeth. Then when it was time
to pay, he opened his window & asked me
which car was mine. I pointed to the worst car
on the block. It looked like it had been
in a wreck. He asked me if I was sure
that was mine, because he had seen it there
for a while. I told him business was so bad
that I couldn't afford to drive it, so I
left it in a safe neighborhood. He hardly
charged me anything. Then I walked back to my
        Cadillac.

WEDDING GIFT

I gave your cousin a big check
for his wedding present, Father said.
He must have liked taking my money,
because he's getting married again.
Now I have to give him another gift.
If I give him less than what I
gave him the first time, he'll think
I'm passing judgment on his marriage
& that I think it won't last. So
I have to give him the exact same sum.
I just hope he doesn't make a habit
out of getting married. It's an easy way
of getting gifts, but I can think
of a lot of better ways to make money.

THE DUCKS WERE GETTING ALONG

We walked through the park. You
said that you hated bringing up
the subject again, but that I don't
meet your needs. I found myself
listening to the ducks. All they
said was quack, quack, quack. But
at least it wasn't aimed at me.

REDECORATION

You said you loved me,
my penis in your hand
was the proof, but then your wrist
got tired & your eyes wandered.
You wanted to move my dresser to another corner,
throw out my desk, replace my bookshelf
with cartons. You made me feel
like a stranger in my own room.

RELUCTANT TRAVELER

The only time you got out of Queens,
my therapist said, was when you saw
your girlfriend in Brooklyn. But you
can't rely on your romances to take
the place of traveling. You should
go to another city all by yourself.
Because what'll happen if you fall
for someone who lives on the same block?
You may never get out of the neighborhood.

ALL IS FAIR IN LOVE

You keep assuming that if you love
a woman, my therapist said, she'll have
to love you. But love isn't like
a Monopoly board game where each player
follows a prescribed set of instructions.
People do what they want to do.
So if she decided not to see you
this weekend without giving you
a good reason, you can't
tell her she's not playing
by the rules, because there are none.

KNOWING YOUR ROLE

Your girlfriend is wrong to be always telling you
what to do, my therapist said. I'm your therapist,
but I never tell you what to do. All I do
is show you your options. You can either
do A or B. Or you can do what you mostly do,
C, which is nothing. I'm smart enough
to know that if I told you what to do
& you did it & it didn't work out,
you'd be mad at me. It's better for me
if you only have yourself to blame.
I don't know why she wants to take over
my role & try to be your therapist.
I always respected her role. I
never once tried to be your girlfriend.

I'M A BELIEVER

You kept telling everyone that the world
is divided, my therapist said,
into two types of people—those
who believe in love at first sight
& those who don't. You sounded
like Neil Diamond singing, "I'm
a believer." But if the recipient
of your romanticism, your girlfriend,
was getting tired of hearing it,
& stopped being a believer,
then that meant you were
singing the same song too long.

AFTER THE BREAKUP

It seemed like breaking up with you
wasn't satisfying enough for her,
my therapist said, so she felt
compelled to keep calling to tell
you why she did it. But if
the driver of a truck ran over
my foot, I wouldn't be interested
in what went through his mind
when the incident happened. I'd
just be thinking about my foot.

AVOIDING AGGRAVATION

When you don't hear from her for a while,
my therapist said, you shouldn't think
that you're missing out on sex,
but rather that you're avoiding
being aggravated. She's better
at giving you a tough time
than she is at sleeping with you.
She has to see you to sleep with you.
But she can give you a tough time
any time she wants. All she has
to do is just pick up the phone.

TOO MUCH FOR HER TO HANDLE

She was having sex with you once
a week, my therapist said. Then
she switched it to once every other week.
That's not going from less to more.
That's going in the opposite direction.
It seems like sleeping with you each week
was too much for her to handle,
so she wants to sleep with you less.
That's not a good prognosis. I
know that in some marriages the couple
only have sex once in two weeks.
But that has no bearing in your case.
You're not married to each other.

TAKING A SLOW TRAIN

You shouldn't keep telling your girlfriend,
my therapist said, that she needs to be
in therapy. You might think that you're
trying to help her, but she sees it
as an insult. Not everyone needs therapy.
Just like not everyone likes to take planes,
some people prefer to take their time
& travel by train. And she may not want
to get rid of her anger right away. It
seems like she's getting too much enjoyment
out of it by directing it at you.

A CHANGE OF DREAMS

You keep having the same dream,
my therapist said, where a woman
dumps cold water on your head.
And I think the dream is telling you
that you better wake up to the fact
that your relationship is ending, so
it won't be such a shock. And
the one good thing that'll happen
when you do break up with her is
you'll be able to dream about something else.

GIVE ME A TICKET FOR A JET PLANE

Just like an alcoholic keeps moving
to new towns, my therapist said,
because he thinks the move will help
him stop drinking, you started having
long-distance romances. But the only
lasting thing you're getting out of them
is a lot of frequent flyer miles.
She liked the idea of you traveling
all those miles just to see her,
but once you were there you weren't
any different from the men she
already knew. And they were more available.

THE VALUE OF TIME

If you argue with her one hour
a week, my therapist said,
that might not seem like much.
But if you do it every week
for an entire year, that's
fifty-two hours of arguing.
That's more than two full days.
You could have used that time
spending a weekend together
in the Poconos, but I don't
recommend you doing that; you'd
just argue about which hotel to stay in.

PHONE DATE

Telling you she's going to be home
on a certain night, my therapist said,
then not being there when you call
is setting you up for disappointment.
It's like a mousetrap with cheese.
I don't know if you had mice
in your apartment. I did. Sometimes
they don't nibble at the bait.
That's what you should do.
Don't call her for a while.

SQUASHED TOES

The problem with being in love with someone
who's not in love with you, my therapist said,
is that you're thinking in capital letters
& she's only thinking in lowercase ones.
So when she steps on your foot, you wonder if
she was saying that at times she has to step
on you to get what she wants, but you shouldn't
take it personally. But for her it probably
just meant that your foot was in the way.

BRUSHING YOUR TEETH

When I went to the bathroom, Mother said,
I noticed your toothbrush wasn't wet,
which meant you didn't brush your teeth again.
And when you get a wife, she won't have to look
at your toothbrush to tell if you brushed
your teeth. She'll just smell your breath,
& if your mouth stinks, she won't want
to get near you. And if you're not able to kiss,
there's a good chance your marriage will collapse.

THE CONTEST

I'm sure you're saying bad things about me,
Mother said. You get together with your friends
& have a contest to see who had the worst mother.
And the only reason why you win
is because you have a very good imagination.
They're telling the truth. You're making everything up.
I'm a very good mother. Everyone thinks so,
except you. But you're too emotionally involved
with me to be a good judge. If I tell you
to do anything, you get red. That color
doesn't look good on your face.

WHY THE VIOLIN IS BETTER

I don't know why you want to play
the drums, Mother said. They won't prepare
you for anything in life, except how to be
a garbageman & bang cans around. But if
you keep studying the violin, you could be
in an orchestra. It'll teach you how
to dress. You'll have to wear a suit
or a tuxedo. And you'll learn how
to play in harmony with other instruments,
like the trombone, which will help you
get along better with me. Because
quite frankly you've been living
in this house like you're the soloist,
making a lot of noise but never stopping
for a moment to see if I wanted to blow my horn.

MUSEUM

I went through your things like a detective.
I tried to find out why you stopped liking me.
I couldn't narrow it down to one reason.

One of my drawers is filled with your stuff.
I wanted to get a larger apartment,
& have a whole room for you.
It would have become like a museum.
Your absence would have gone on display.

Your picture is in the closet.
It's next to the books I have read,
& don't intend to read again.

TWO-SECOND KISS

Kissing her was like
biting into a juicy orange
& getting a mouthful of seeds.

BUMPING INTO AN EX-LOVER

I've been meaning to call you,
she said, but you know how life is—
just when I'm about to do it,
something happens to delay it.
I'm on my way to a meditation center.
I don't really like sitting
on a cold wooden floor. And the chants
are all in a foreign language.
Sometimes I find myself thinking
about you, but that's not to say
I don't think about other things,
like when the service will be over,
so I can talk to people & have fun.

THE PILLS I'M GIVING YOU

You should take medication, my therapist said.
You need to think of yourself as having diabetes.
A diabetic has to take insulin because
he can't metabolize sugar. And you got the
     wrong type
of attention when you were growing up,
so you lack love. You only have so much
energy, & you're using all yours up
feeling sad. But if you take tranquilizers,
you'll have energy left over to do what you want.
No one has to know you're taking them.
You can swallow them when people aren't
looking. And if they knew what you were
taking, they'd ask you if they could have some, too.

I WANT TO BE SEDATED

The good thing about the Valium
I'm prescribing for you, my therapist said,
is that you can break each pill in half.
You can take half just before you meet your date,
& the other half in the middle of it.
And don't worry if you don't have
a good time & it ends earlier
than you planned. I'm also giving
you a pill that'll make you sleep.

YOU WEREN'T BLEEDING

I'm giving you the book *What Every Teenager
Needs to Know About Sex,* my therapist said.
You should have gotten it seven years ago,
but since no one gave it to you, I'm
giving it to you now. Children from families
where sex was never discussed have
the most problems. Your parents probably
thought you'd pick up all this information
by yourself, but if you're dependent
on friends to tell you the facts of life,
you're bound to get a lot of misinformation.
The first time you ejaculated you thought
you were bleeding. That'd never have
happened if you had read the first chapter.

NO NEED TO TELL ALL

Every dog has its day, my therapist said,
but you had your week. It's too bad
we only have one hour together, because
it seems like you have a lot to tell me.
But you don't need to tell me everything.
You can leave out one or two things,
so if nothing happens to you next week,
you'll still have something to say.

SAFETY VALVE

In the outside world if you yell
at people, my therapist said, there are
repercussions. Someone might yell back.
But in my office you can scream
at me, & I'll stay calm. You can do
in here what you can't do outside. But
the only favor I'll ask of you
is please don't make any noises that sound
like I'm strangling you, because I
have a new patient waiting outside.

BREAKING DOWN

Everyone has a nervous breakdown
at least once in his life, my therapist said,
so you're lucky to be having yours now
while you're still young enough to be
able to do something about it. It's a lot
harder to handle when you're older
& have a wife & family. You couldn't
just take a year off. So when the friends
you knew in high school are having
their breakdowns in their forties & fifties,
you'll be able to breathe a sigh of relief,
because you already got yours over with.

BASKETBALL AFICIONADO

Whatever you tell me in therapy
is confidential, my therapist said.
I don't even mention it to my husband.
He only cares about sports. If you
were a basketball player, he'd like
to know how you got ready
for a big game. But he
wouldn't care how many girlfriends
dropped you, or how many times
you dropped someone. He's not
interested in those kinds of scores.

QUICK SALE

Trying to find a therapist,
my therapist said, is like shopping
for pants. You can't always buy
the first pair you try on. But
you & I seemed to have hit it off
the first time we met. When you
told me about your parents
& your girlfriends, I took your side.
But now that you're attacking me,
you can't expect me to be so sympathetic.

THE CLOCK ON THE TABLE

Your time is up, my therapist said.
Next week we'll continue where you
left off. Or maybe something so exciting
will happen to you that you won't
even want to finish this story. Think
of this hour with me as your private film.
You're the director. You can show me
whatever you want. But I'm not
a passive spectator. I'm a therapist.
I'll stop you if you keep repeating yourself.

BETTER THAN A FRIEND

You shouldn't tell everyone that you're
in therapy, my therapist said. Some people
might think you're crazy. If
someone asks why you go to the city
at the same time each week, you should
just tell him that you have an appointment
with a friend, which is not really a lie,
because I'm your friend. But I'm also
so much more. You can insult me, & I'll
never get mad. I'll just say that you're
transferring again. I'll never leave you,
but you can leave me. One day you'll
tell me that you don't need to see me anymore,
& instead of being mad, I'll be happy,
because that'll mean you're cured. But
I wouldn't advise you to do that
in the near future. You still have problems.

EARLY INTERVENTION

I didn't yell at you, Mother said.
I just raised my voice a little. That's
a big difference. You make me seem
like an ogre, but the truth is, I'm
very concerned about you. You have
no ambition. You don't look for a job.
When you were little, I tried to discourage you
from talking to yourself. People might think
you were crazy. Now I know I shouldn't
have said anything. I should have
just let you be crazy, so by the time
you got to be this age, you'd have grown out of it.

WRONG SHIRT

I don't know what was on your sister's mind,
Mother said, when she bought your father
this shirt, but she wasn't thinking about him.
It's his size, but it doesn't match
his personality. It's much too bland.
It's for someone who doesn't know
what he wants to do in life.
That's why he's giving it to you.

IGNORANT PEOPLE

No matter how nice you act toward strangers,
Mother said, there'll always be some who won't
like you because you're from the wrong religion.
You're Jewish. So since you're never going
to please them, you might as well try to please me.
You should get into the habit of making your bed.
And just because people hate you doesn't mean
that you should take it personally. They're
just ignorant. Hitler was stupid, too. If you
look at photographs of him, you'll notice
he wore boots even during the summer.

FROM SHOES TO SEX

She said that she doesn't want to have sex
because she's afraid it'll get in the way
of the relationship. I said that it'll only
get in the way if she lets it. She said
that it has already interfered with our conversation.
She was talking about buying shoes, which she
knows a lot about, but now I'm forcing her
to talk about sex, which she knows less about.

ALIKE & DIFFERENT

We're both Jewish, she said, so we
have that in common. We're both tall.
We must have at least one hundred
other things in common. But the only thing
that might make us a little different
is that I'm a talker & you're not,
so I'm going to shut up right now
& let you finish the conversation.

BAD TRACK RECORDS

She didn't have a good track record,
my therapist said. She got divorced
two times, & the only reason she
didn't get divorced from the third guy
she had a kid with was because
they never got married. You don't
have a good track record, either.
That's why I thought you & she
would have a lot in common. But
a big difference is that she's still mad
at her ex-lovers. You already forgave yours.

GOING FOR THE HIGH STAKES

I think the reason you were so intent
on marrying her, my therapist said,
was you wanted to keep the stakes high
to make it more interesting. It was
an either/or situation. Either you were
going to marry her or it wasn't
going to work out. There was no
in between. You should look at it
from the positive side. You got half
of what you wanted. It didn't work out.

KILLING THE SONG

If the reason someone gave for breaking up
with me, my therapist said, was "the thrill
is gone," I'd be annoyed, too. You'd
hope she'd be a little more inventive
& come up with an original excuse & not
the title of a song. Because what she
has done is kill that song for you. Now
whenever you hear it, you won't be
able to enjoy it, but you'll keep thinking,
How could she say something as trite
as that to me, I should have said it first.

TWO PLANNED KIDS

When she told you that she wanted
two kids, my therapist said, & she was
looking at you while she was saying it,
I'd also have thought that she wanted
them with me. There was no other guy
in the room at the time. But now
she says she wanted two kids
with someone else. She doesn't
know who that person is yet.
But she just knows it's not you.
I feel sorry for him. He
doesn't know what he's walking into.

REPEAT

You never seemed crazy about her,
my therapist said. Your feelings
toward her were always lukewarm.
Being a spectator isn't a bad thing—
there are a lot of plays I want to see—
but if your relationship reminds you
too much of a bad television show
that you think you've seen before
& can't wait to turn off,
then maybe you shouldn't be in it.

BAD FORECAST

I hate to be the voice of doom,
my therapist said, but I knew
your relationship wasn't going to work out.
She had three children by three different
men. Her last boyfriend was a junkie.
I tried to overlook those facts, but
I kept feeling like a weatherman
predicting a hurricane. I knew
I wouldn't be responsible for all the damage,
but I felt bad about it anyway.

PUTTING YOUR FOOT DOWN

If you have to wait until she
tells you the relationship is over,
my therapist said, to realize that she
isn't as pretty & smart as you
thought she was, then you are
letting your imagination take over.
You have to rely more on your instincts.
They're like the brakes on a car.
You're supposed to use them to stop
yourself from getting into danger.
But you seem to use them only
after you have the accident.

SWEET THINGS

She wasn't giving you a private language,
my therapist said. If she said *honey*,
it wasn't meant as a term of endearment,
but that she was talking about food.
She wasn't whispering sweet things
into your ears, but only using them
as erogenous zones, & once
she stopped sleeping with you,
they no longer had a purpose.

SEX MAY NOT MEAN MUCH

You were putting more into the relationship
than she was, my therapist said. All she
was putting in was sex. It seemed
like a lot at the time, because you hadn't
slept with anyone for a year, but
it wasn't. And she might not have slept
with you for the reason you wanted—
that she was in love with you—but
because she wanted her ex-boyfriend
to know she was sleeping with someone else.

TOO MUCH STRATEGY

If the success of the relationship depends
on strategy, my therapist said, on thinking
if I only did this & didn't do that,
then it's not working. You should be
able to put your arms around her
without worrying about the consequences.
If you turn on your TV, it plays.
When you shut it off, it stops playing.
She needs to be more consistent.
After you sleep together she
shouldn't be kicking you out of the house.

GETTING CLOSER TO FATHER

I want you to take violin lessons, Mother said,
so you'll get closer to your father. Whenever
I see you two together, you never seem
to talk about anything. He doesn't talk
to me much, either, but we're married,
so we don't have to talk. We have
other ways to communicate. But if you
studied the violin, he could help you
with your lessons, because he knows how
to play that instrument. This way, if
you still don't want to talk
to him, you don't have to. You two
could just play a duet instead.

MOTHER TALKS TO THE DEAD

When we went to visit Grandmother's grave,
you told me to look at the other tombstones
& find the person who has been dead the longest.
You said that you had to be alone because
there were certain things that you needed to tell her,
& if I was bothering you, you might forget
some of them. Just when I found someone
who had died fifty years before I was born,
you said it was time to leave. You
said that you told her about me. I asked
if you told her about all the good things
that I did, like the time I walked the old woman
across the street. You said you told her
the truth, that you could only tell lies
to people who were living, but you couldn't
lie to the dead because you didn't know what
         they knew.

SHOPPING FOR CEMETERY PLOTS

Mother said I hurt my father's feelings
when I refused the cemetery plot
he bought me for a birthday present.
She said it's not the kind of thing
that's easy to return. He had to talk them
into taking it back. Now he won't get me
another one even if I beg for it.
It's up to me to buy my own. I'll be sorry
when I find out how much they cost.
If I go shopping for one years before
I need it, I can get a much better deal.
It isn't something I'll outgrow.

TOO MUCH WINE

She didn't have any curtains,
so I had to wait for it to get dark
before I could try to seduce her.
We drank wine. It helped
the time pass. Then I took off
her blouse. But before I could
do anything else, she threw up
all over the bed. She said
I should go. She was feeling sick.
I felt frustrated on the ride home.
I tried to cheer myself up.
Things could have been worse.
She could have thrown up on me.

THE NEXT ONE

Promise me that when I die, she said,
you'll go out with other women.
Don't make me into a memory, because
I'll be watching you from heaven,
& I don't want to be bored. I'll
be curious to see what they'll look like.
Don't go for an exact copy of me.
You could use someone a little taller.

BALL & CHAIN

I walked by a couple in the park
who were so busy kissing & hugging
that they didn't even see me. We
were once like that, your hand
on my lap in a crowded subway car,
like a dog owner who wouldn't let go of the leash.

PUTTING YOURSELF BACK
TOGETHER AGAIN

It wasn't your choice to break up
with her, my therapist said. It's
almost like you're being split
into two. One of you wants
to get back with her. The other
wants nothing to do with her.
But it's not like you're
a Humpty-Dumpty who fell off
the wall & couldn't be put back
together again. You already
have a date with someone else.

GETTING CLOSER TO THE AISLE

The more you tell people you're going
to get married, my therapist said,
the more you think it'll come true.
But now when friends see you, all they ask
is, Are you married yet? And when you
tell them you're not but that you will be soon,
they'll ask why you've been putting it off.
But when you tell them you're now going
to marry someone else, not the woman
you were telling them about, they're going
to get confused. It's like they need
a scorecard just to keep track of you.

NOT EVERYONE IS CRAZY

Just because your last girlfriend was crazy,
my therapist said, doesn't mean that all the women
you meet will be crazy. There have to be
sane women around. I'm an example of one.
I doubt that I exist in a vacuum. There
must be others like me. I think you want
to convince yourself that the women you're meeting
are crazy, so if the relationship doesn't last,
it won't be that much of a disappointment.
But there are a lot of reasons besides her craziness
why you & she won't be able to get along together.
It may be as simple as she just doesn't like you.

CONFUSING ONE WITH THE OTHER

You're going out with someone new,
my therapist said. But then you keep
walking past your ex-girlfriend's house.
In a kosher household you're supposed
to keep the silverware you use with meat
separate from the ones you use with dairy.
But you're not being able to do that
with your relationships. You're going out
with one, but you keep thinking about the other.

UNLIKELY TO SUCCEED

It was a bad omen, my therapist said,
when she told you that she thought
the relationship wasn't going to last.
You might expect to hear that
after you had your first fight,
but for her to say that on the first date
means she's either being too pessimistic
or she has too much inside information.

ALLERGIC REACTION

It seemed that the less you liked her,
my therapist said, the more allergic
you got to her cat. When she was
nice to you, you'd put it on your lap,
& never had a reaction. But when
she started to treat you badly, you'd
wheeze & cough all night, & she couldn't
sleep. She reached the point where she
had to decide between you or her cat.
And you were the one she let go.
Because even though it didn't listen
to her, either, it never kept her up at night.

THREE THINGS COULD HAPPEN

When you see her this weekend,
my therapist said, three things can
happen. One, you sleep together.
Two, you don't sleep together, but
you still get close. Or three,
it falls apart. But if you just kept
talking to her on the phone & never
arranged this visit, you wouldn't have
had so many options, but would
have been like a student who didn't
know anything on a multiple-choice test
& kept marking the box "None of the above."

SHE DID IT HER WAY

There's no correct way to break up
with someone, my therapist said. I
don't believe Emily Post wrote
about it. Your girlfriend could
have done it in a nicer way.
For some reason she decided to do it
in person. I know you'd have
preferred her to do it over the phone.
That way, you could have hung up, & she
wouldn't have known how you reacted.
She wouldn't have seen you try not to cry.

ONLY YOU HEAR
THE WEDDING BELLS

Right now you think she loves you,
my therapist said. You're in your
manic stage. But I predict
that by tomorrow you'll be
depressed again when you realize
that if she liked you she'd have
tried to see you, & not have kept putting you off.
I hate to be the bearer of bad tidings.
I wish I could tell you that one day
you'll marry her. But you have
to face the fact that she's not
going to marry someone she never sees.

FRIEND OR PARTNER

Right now you have a fifty percent chance
of sleeping with her, my therapist said.
But the more you see her, the more
the percentage will go down, because
she'll be so used to not sleeping with you
that when you broach the subject again,
she won't know how to react. So if
you intend to sleep with her, you better
do it soon. But if you just want
to be her friend, then the percentages are
already in your favor, & there's no rush.

KNOWLEDGE

In my day, Mother said, a kiss was
a commitment. If a man kissed
a woman, that meant he was willing
to catch her cold. Nowadays when
a man gets a cold, he doesn't know
who he got it from. It could
have been from his wife, or from
his girlfriend. Divorce used to be
a dirty word, & now it's called
a learning experience. You're supposed
to learn everything you need to know
about the woman before you marry her.

FORTY DOLLARS A WORD

The rabbi said beautiful words about
your mother at her funeral, Father said.
I was impressed until I got the bill.
He charged me a thousand dollars. I
figured that each beautiful word
cost me about forty dollars. If I
knew it was going to cost me that much,
I'd have said them myself. But he's
a rabbi. I'm not. So I paid & shut up.

J. C. PENNEY

One time I was waiting on line
to see a buyer, Father said. Another
salesman got in front of me. When
I said something, he kicked my bag
of samples. I gave him such a wallop
that I'd have broken my knuckles
if they weren't already broken. He
punched me in the nose. Our blood
got on the floor. Then J. C. Penney
stepped between us, grabbed us
by our collars, & kicked us out.
He told us never to come back. You
could imagine the look on our faces.
We were both six-footers, & he was
only a little guy. We were shocked.
We never knew that he existed. We
thought he was just the name of a store.

MY VERSION OF IT

You told your friend that we were lovers,
but I only remember sharing a cheese blintze
with you, & you took the bigger half.

YOU NEVER KNEW ME

You look at a cortesa tree,
see nothing. You walk
toward it, & then eight wrens fly out.

THE DEFENSE SPEAKS

You can't accuse me of making you
depressed, my therapist said, because
you were depressed before you even knew me.
I could tell when you first walked in today
that it was going to be one of those sessions
where you put me on trial again,
& become the judge & jurors. The
only thing I'll say in my defense
is that I can't be as bad
as you're making me out to be
or you'd have stopped seeing me.

ONLY SHE KNOWS WHERE HE LIVES

When you were in love with her,
my therapist said, you didn't worry
why her last lover left. But
as you & she got into more altercations,
you slowly found yourself taking his side.
And when you broke up with her,
you realized how smart he was
for ending the relationship faster
than you did. And you'd have liked
to talk to him to compare notes.
But that won't ever happen. She's
never going to give you his address.

SPEAKING IN QUOTES

She doesn't use authentic language,
my therapist said. For example, she'll say,
"I have trouble making commitments."
You already know that. It took
you a few weeks just to make
a first date. What she should be
saying instead is, "Help." Then you
both could do something about it.
I hate to use hackneyed expressions,
like she does, but she needs
"to put everything on the table."
At this point in the relationship
she hasn't even put out the silverware.

THE LIKING GAME

You're always laying your cards on the table,
my therapist said. You're always telling
the woman you like her before she has
the chance to say she likes you. Sometimes
your approach is going to work. And
at other times you'll end up falling
flat on your face. You have
to accept the fact that not every woman
is going to like you. I happen
to like you a lot. But I'm not
going out with you, so I don't really count.

MATCH MADE IN HEAVEN

Telling her that you thought God sent
her to you, my therapist said, is putting
her under a lot of pressure. If she
breaks up with you, she'll feel she's
committing an irreligious act. And
if God sent her, then He wasn't a very good
matchmaker. He needs to send you someone
you have something in common with.

GIRLFRIEND CANDIDATE

Your last girlfriend reminded me of Clinton,
my therapist said. He's not good
as a President, but he's great as a candidate.
And she also made you a lot of promises,
but she never delivered. She never
promised you health care, but she did
say you could always stay with her.
Then she reneged on that. Now that
you know what she has to offer,
you should let her campaign somewhere else.

THE DATING POOL

You should stop going out with women
you meet in group therapy, my therapist said.
You're bound to meet a saner one at a dance.
And if you don't like her, you don't have
to see her again. But if you break up with someone
in the group, you're stuck having to sit
next to her every week. And instead
of working on solving your problems, you'll
be talking about her, & she'll be talking
about you. You can tell a lot about a woman
by where you met. If you met her
in a museum, then she must love art,
but if you met her in group therapy,
then you have to expect her to have problems.

WANTING TO KNOW

The only way you can find out why
she doesn't want to go out with you,
my therapist said, is to ask her, but
since she's not returning your calls,
you may never know. I'm a woman,
so I'm closer to her temperament
than you are, but I wouldn't presume
to speak for her. But finding out
may not necessarily help you with
the next woman you meet. Not all women
are going to reject you for the same reason.

NEEDING TO KNOW MORE

Just telling me that the woman you recently met
was nice, my therapist said, is not giving me
enough information to work with. Sometimes
you give me only the minimal essentials.
Then you blame me if it doesn't work out.
But my advice is only as good as the information
I get. If you tell me she ate dinner, I won't
know much about her. But if you tell me what food
she ordered, I might be able to give you some clues.

LENDING OUT BOOKS

You're always giving, my therapist said.
You have to learn how to take. Whenever
you meet a woman, the first thing you do
is lend her your books. You think she'll
have to see you again in order to return them.
But what happens is, she doesn't have the time
to read them, & she's afraid if she sees you again
you'll expect her to talk about them, & will
want to lend her even more. So she
cancels the date. You end up losing
a lot of books. You should borrow hers.

TAKING THE FIFTH

She's acting too much like Oliver North,
my therapist said. You ask her,
"What's wrong with our relationship?"
She refuses to answer. You know she
knows more than she's letting on. And
you can tell that she's still going to do
the exact same things that made you
mad at her in the first place, because
in her mind she's convinced she's right.

FORGIVING YOUR EX

Jesus said, "Forgive them Lord, for they know
not what they do," my therapist said.
And He was right. They don't. When
she slept with you, she didn't know
that you were going to fall in love
with her. And when she broke up
with you, she didn't know that you'd
have to see me more. And yet you can't hold
her responsible for your becoming depressed.
There was just a lot she didn't know.

MOVING FORWARD

You've made great improvements,
my therapist said, since you first
started seeing me. You still have
some trouble getting along with people,
but you get along better with me.
On your first visit you were
uncommunicative. Then you started
to open up. Now I look forward
to talking with you. I predict
that you'll soon get a girlfriend.
But whatever you do, don't make the mistake
of thinking that talking to her is the same
as talking to me. She might not be
interested in listening to all your problems.

Hal Sirowitz's first collection, *Mother Said,*
was published in 1996. He has been awarded
a National Endowment for the Arts Fellowship. He has
appeared on MTV's *Spoken Word Unplugged* and at
the Lollapalooza Festival. And he has been featured
on PBS's *The United States of Poetry* and on
NPR's *All Things Considered.*
He lives in Flushing, New York.